Where Horizons Go

WHERE HORIZONS GO

POEMS BY RHINA P. ESPAILLAT

NEW ODYSSEY PRESS
KIRKSVILLE, MISSOURI

First New Odyssey edition published 1998
Copyright © 1998 Thomas Jefferson University Press
Printed in the United States of America

Author photo by Brian Gonye

Cover illustration is *Woman reading a letter at an open window* by Jan Vermeer, reproduced by permission of Erich Lessing/Art Resource, NY.

03 02   5 4 3

Library of Congress Cataloging-in-Publication Data

Espaillat, Rhina P. (Rhina Polonia), 1932–
    Where horizons go : poems / by Rhina P. Espaillat.—1st New Odyssey ed.
        p.   cm.
    ISBN 0-943549-55-8 (alk. paper). — ISBN 0-943549-56-6 (pbk. : alk. paper)
    I. Title
PS3555.S535W48   1998
811'.54—dc21   98-23273
                                                                      CIP

New Odyssey Press is an imprint of Truman State University Press at Truman State University in Kirksville, Missouri 63501 (*http://www2.truman.edu/tjup*).

The paper in this publication meets or exceeds the minimum requirements of the American National Standard—Permanence of Paper for Printed Library Materials, ANSI Z39.48 (1984).

To the members of the Powow River Poets,
with my thanks for their encouragement and good company,
and most especially to Len Krisak,
who devoted a great deal of intelligent attention to the manuscript.
This book would not have been possible without his insight, his honesty,
or his patience.

Contents

ACKNOWLEDGMENTS

MY THANKS to the following publications, where several of the poems in this manuscript first appeared or are scheduled to appear:

America for "Weighing In," *Blue Unicorn* for "The Quetzal," *Caprice* for "Six of One," *Defined Providence* for "Driving Through It" and "Song," *Eagle-Tribune* for "For My Great-Great Grandson the Space Pioneer," *The Formalist* for "Almost," *Hellas* for "January," *The Lyric* for "Falling" and "In Absentia," *Medicinal Purposes* for "Neighbors," "Poetry Reading," and "If You Ask Me," *Northeast* for "Bilingual/Bilingüe," *Orbis,* U.K., for Map Lesson" and "Roach," *Pivot* for "Parallax" and "Why Publish?," *Poetry* for "Last Day," *Poetry Digest* for "Bread" and "For Evan, Who Says I Am Too Tidy," *Poetry NY* for "Map Lesson," *Sparrow* for "Calendar," "Gravida," and "Quandary," *The Tennessee Review* for "Ash Wednesday" and "The Prodigal Son Goes Over Notes for His Memoirs," and *Voices International* for "Rainy Sunday."

Several of the poems in this manuscript have won recent awards:

"Children Blowing Bubbles" and "Sacrament" received the 1996 Annual Award from *The Plum Review;* "Map Lesson" and "Roach" received awards from *Orbis* magazine in 1996; "Almost" was one of eleven finalists in the 1996 Howard Nemerov Sonnet Contest.

IF YOU ASK ME

"If you ask me," said the snake, "this couple's doomed:
they started naked, not a thing to need,
a thing to wonder at, since orders boomed
over the speaker. Every day they weed
a little, see what's ripe and pluck it off,
eat this, no don't eat that. Now I'm not blind:
I see her fidget with her hair and cough
that nervous cough; she's bored out of her mind.
I see him gawk at birds and flap in vain;
then his blank eyes cloud over with the sky
and circle his estate, so green, so plain.
She's ripe to risk herself; they need to die;
unbanished, he's an ornament, a brute.
We're neighbors; I'll go visiting, with fruit."

CURRENT

Coiled to spring, newly unplugged from the homely
percolator, you watch me with tense nostril-
eyes that rivet like fangs, your small motionless
head malignant and useful, angry god that
reached for me once in childhood through a hairpin
probing the wall's secrets, sudden and smoother
than sex or whiskey, a licking all over
by fire, a rod of ice in the marrow.
And afterward I hid night after night, but
ah, you found me in dreams, flicking your quick tongue
lewdly from the safety of familiar things;
you crouch in my walls; you ripple your braid of
muscle among dark leaves in the mind's garden.

13

BARKER

You say you want adventure and romance?
Crave feats of daring? scenes of perils dire?
Come to the sideshow: that's your only chance.

In the big tent, glitter and elegance
go sequined far above you on the wire:
you say you want adventure and romance,

but from the stands you strain for a mere glance
of either as they clamber high and higher.
Come to the sideshow, it's your only chance

to test the shackles on those flagellants
who do the tricks in them that you, the buyer,
have said you want. Adventure and romance

are not for those who view them through a trance
under cold glass, like jewels to admire:
come to the sideshow for your only chance

to join the paraplegic in his dance,
lunch with the starving geek who eats the fire
you say you want. Adventure and romance

are never far: look in this mirror, sans
pity, and voilà, your heart's desire.
You say you want adventure and romance?
Come to the sideshow: we're your only chance.

ALMOST

I peer inside it to make sure, and yes,
this is your car beside mine in the lot,
your jacket on the seat, your children's mess
of blankets and stuffed animals: I spot
a letter to be mailed, a shopping list.
Not spotting you, at last I drive away,
framing my joke; how cleverly you missed
lugging your mother's bags on shopping day!
And think how easily—by blindest chance—
this cell or that could have flicked elsewhere, failed
to clasp in that first moment of the dance
that life begins with, how you could have sailed
out of all possibility, downstream,
lost to my flesh forever, like a dream.

In Absentia

Blue-penciled from our script, my stillborn brother,
have you found room on some congenial stage
less brutal than live flesh, or do you hover
above each page

as I grind through commitments on my tour?
I play to scant applause, and think of you
sometimes, who in your one brief scene stayed pure
but missed your cue.

Good to a fault, unflawed as any naught,
you are the unheard melody, the light
too far to work by where we shadows squat
in our cave night.

Type-cast and contract-bound to this one face
I speak my lines through, whether right or wrong,
I've envied you your place.
But not for long.

MAP LESSON

My grandson takes my hand and puts it down
on one coast, then the other. Let's go east
to west, I tell him, starting from our town:
straddle the Mississippi, shaggy beast
back dull with flood silt; here's where the plains
spill out to scrubby foothills, rise to looming
mountains that snag clouds and keep the rains
from—touch this patch—desert; beyond, consuming
California tide by tide, another ocean.
He tries the route alone now, finger, eye
transmuting letters into highway, motion
of water, hum of cities wheeling by.
I watch him take possession, claim the land
perilous inch by inch. I take his hand.

CALENDAR

Clean as a winter field, the year begins:
page after page of days untouched, still clear
as snow beside those roads you never took.
You test it with your thought, as with the skin's
tentative appetite, hunger and fear
together in the nerve, time's pristine book
still eloquent in its rich silence. Look
how each blank square leaves you four sides to steer
between, without a signpost; how each row
of seven multiplies, tier after tier,
like chorus girls. Imagination spins…
and then recoils: you print the text you know:
doctor's appointments, birthdays, come and go
of friends, those old delights, those trusty sins.

January

There's the horizon still in place,
gray ribbon threaded taut and lean
through those bare twigs that summer-long
hid it behind a scrim of green.

I liked it green—as well as bare—
my quarter-acre in the sun;
I would not dress it otherwise
than seasons in their turn have done,

but do give thanks that sultry weather
of much to feel and less to know
gives way, after a time, to this
clear view of where horizons go.

Haiku

In our bare maple
a minyan of crows looking
for something to bless

Intricate river
in winter light Twig to root
flowing underground

Sundial deep in white
all day long reads exactly
half past January

Thinking of old friends
Black iron stove Slow fire
talking to itself

Keys on a rusty
key ring Old conversations
Nobody home now

This mother-of-pearl
morning sealed with frost Ah but
two crows on the fence

ASH WEDNESDAY

Now every flame sinks lowest, in the hearth,
in aging blood, and in the shriveled bough.
Brutal in white, wind-armies of the north
besiege both soul and sense with silence. Now
paw prints grow faint and vanish in the swirl,
margin and pond in the crow's eye congeal
to one bleak zero, and the snake lies curled
under the iron stillness of the field.
How shall all this be warmed to rise again,
out of such bitter dreams, or none at all,
into green hope? Come speak the word, as when
the stars sang the first echo of your call,
or clay first breathed, or on that fourth daybreak,
Lazarus, at your bidding, stirred awake.

CHILDREN BLOWING BUBBLES

Children blowing bubbles on the back porch
wave them over the railing, where they wobble
in windless heat toward roundness, or lengthen,
dragging the garden slowly upside down
through mauve and blue, popping to sudden droplets.

Perfect either way, whether suspended
oracular overhead or vanished wetly,
they multiply, multiply into the trees,
swift and still by turns, to the cries of the children
whose arms and faces drip with creation.

An easy summer poem, all metaphor,
all motion: if I were half the poet,
I would leave it unworded, as they do,
lose it unmourned, let the sun slide and burst
a thousand times, this once, without regret.

SOLSTICE

Now in our maple a dove is whooing;
caught in the branches, the wind is warm;
somewhere heaven is plotting storm
and the bird's undoing.

Now in the flame of its petals burning,
sunflower praises the gift of sun;
elsewhere petals are all undone,
and the leaves are turning.

MAN RAKING LEAVES

A man is raking leaves. It is October,
still warm this windless afternoon, a good day
for his laborious shuffle through blown russet,
amber and brown gold, between lawn and gutter.

He feels November coming, knows the lyrics
of that dark song it sings in eaves and chimney,
the way it has of stripping his last maple
down to the thinnest shadow. But for now,

the man is raking only those leaves
earliest to fall, in the light shade of others
still there where summer pinned them. He is reading
another message in their easy drifting,

answering with a gesture of his shoulders
pulled back to ease the spine, no longer limber
but willing to bend here in a light like honey
pouring around his body, stroking his body,

the rake, the leaves, the tree that drops them,
the grass they lie on. And he thinks, How simple,
again, again, to make this motion,
to know what October means, to be glad and tired.

NOVEMBER

"We grow accustomed to the Dark—
When Light is put away…"

—Emily Dickinson

How easily beguiled by day and night
our trees, all summer long, clapped their delight,
nodding for what there was, finding it good;
like Him who made them in His youthful mood,
finding in repetition without end,
as in a mirrored face, the perfect friend.

Now taught discrimination by a wind
more critical of trifles, newly thinned,
our maples by degrees withhold applause
until some trumpet blast shall give them cause
to praise, in the vernacular of crows,
if not what summer hoped, what winter knows.

Driving Through It

You want to see, but it's too much, all this
rushing vortex of ash, mother-of-pearl
assault on visibility, ice kiss
splattered to water. Through stampeding swirl
of white gone mad, traffic lopes in and out,
and further off, dragging their veils like brides
left waiting, birches sigh and flail about,
their green composure gone. But here inside
your capsule of not-stillness not-quite-moving,
you focus on the small: a single flake
caught for an instant on the glass, held grooving
its hard route up the windshield, tiny rake
through grainy frost, weeping and disappearing.
What can you do through this but keep on steering.

LAST DAY

At year's end, the garden bare, whatever
lives there locked in the grip of zero, blessed be
habits that keep you warm through iron weather:

Light-led motion from sleep to stove and larder,
clink of dishes, clatter of spoons and forks
arranging themselves like words into ritual order;

Clear pour of water under clotted stems
and swollen arthritic joints of old begonias;
Dusting and sweeping out of rooms;

Froth of soiled wash in baptismal suds
and brisk embrace that leaves it fresh and folded;
The reach between canyons of canned goods,

choosing simple quarry you hunt by proxy;
Hiss and slap of mail through the brass lip
of solitude, inviting life in (but slowly,

not too close, or the trapper's scented
lure will draw you out into danger,
into some false thaw, the cry of the hunted);

By night, the slink into sleep again, turning
in that wound-licking posture flesh remembers,
wanting nothing to come but one more morning.

QUANDARY

The more I think, the less it seems to do
outside of thought, the more of it I find
unfit for daily wear, shabbily less
than what it seems. Whatever I pursue
moves on, until I fall so far behind,
the long parade has passed when I confess
the emperor looks cold in thought's undress.
Or have I missed his finery, made blind
by too much sunstruck gold? I look again,
and yes, he's quite as naked as my mind,
which is his emblem: we are one, we two,
neither what I imagined way back when.
Time to rethink this through, I think; but then,
the more I think the less of it seems true.

BRA

What a good fit! But the label says Honduras:
Alas, I am Union forever, yes, both breasts
and the heart between them committed to U.S. labor.

But such a splendid fit! And the label tells me
the woman who made it, bronze as the breasts now in it,
speaks the language I dream in; I count in Spanish

the pesos she made stitching this breast-divider:
will they go for her son's tuition, her daughter's wedding?
The thought is a lovely fit, but oh, the label!

And oh, those pesos that may be pennies, and hard-earned.
Was it son or daughter who made this, unschooled, unwedded?
How old? Fourteen? Ten? That fear is a tight fit.

If only the heart could be worn like the breast, divided,
nosing in two directions for news of the wide world,
sniffing here and there for justice, for mercy.

How burdened every choice is with politics, guilt,
expensive with duty, heavy as breasts in need of
this perfect fit whose label says Honduras.

THE QUETZAL

Our Costa Rican guide raises both hands
for silence: Do you see it, up above
us, in that crooked branch? Quick flurry of
binoculars; every camera scans
the tracery of humid green that spans
the mud we trudge through. We're afraid to move.
And yet this bird is too aloof for love.
I sight below, from his perch to the man's:

the guide, all rapt attention, who forgot
himself in one long look, El Greco eyes
fixed on this iridescent glow that flies
beyond our reach. Later he tells us what
we cost the Earth, and why the forest dies,
and how the quetzal must, if we will not.

DIVINATION

My friend believes the cards that leap and tumble
deftly through her fingers, believes they tell her
what stakes to set, the profit of each day's gamble.

"Magical thinking," I tease her, and shake my head.
Sheathed in her nimbus of gold she smiles and shuffles,
crosses the Queen of Wands with the House of God.

She believes somewhere the future, that rumor, is real,
as a lost coin is real in a damp cellar
where one on his knees may find it, perhaps the Fool,

these four rising to Judgment from their river,
this dapper Juggler, Force breaking the lion's grip,
or Hermit with his lamp, or those handclasped Lovers.

My credo dwindles to this place, this time.
Outside, our maples shuffle and reshuffle,
without a word of news on what's to come.

They know how to spend suns they cannot pocket,
how to scatter seed between blades of grass.
If they know more than this, they keep their secret.

LUNAR MODULE

This is the one I understand: four legs—
tentative, spindly—splayed as if to test
the ground before some web is spun and eggs,
lapped in their dusty silk, float in the nest.
Or, seen more closely, an ungainly cow
whose comic shanks, still bent to graze the Moon,
leaped all those miles back home to straddle, now,
this concrete meadow. Like a huge cartoon,
it mocks itself for tourists, lets them stroke
antenna horns, chrome tail, udder and flanks.
Those others pose like gods beside this joke,
erect for speed and motion, their bright ranks
striding from what we know into cold blue.
And it may be I understand them too.

FALLING

Whatever is, harbors its own unease.
The spring aches, and the taut line sags to ground.
Green leaves pull skyward, blind roots hunger down
To dark necessities.

Even stirs restless and explodes to odd;
Odd strains for symmetry, limps home to even.
In the light-spangled solitude of heaven
God reels away from God.

And in the heart, born single as a kiss,
Broods the sad other—learner, yearner, dier—
That knows, uncomforted, its one desire
Was not for this.

SIX OF ONE

Christopher, you were headed for the East
when you sailed west with Isabela's trinkets.
Corrigan did it wrong too, but at least
he made it faster. When you crossed the drink, its
reputation wasn't one to scoff at:
it took you ten long weeks, your crew hysteric,
mutinous with dread that they'd drop off at
the world's edge.
              You came through—a feat homeric—
to hail Columbia by a name mistaken
and dub her people "Indians," and went home
to die a poor man's death, alone, forsaken
by king and queen. So all roads lead to Rome,
but Rome's not always where our purpose wends.
Should you regret the trip? Well, that depends.

NEIGHBORS

This cemetery and this parking lot,
each busy being what the other's not:
one greenly still, with marble calligraphic
snippets about the dead, one loud with traffic.
Or not so different, if you look again
at the strict quadrilaterals—some ten
or twelve across, row upon row—
where those who stop eventually also
(after a shift of gears, a shift of tense)
move on, some hour or millennium hence.

I like them close this way, so in cahoots,
one proudly, deeply conscious of its roots,
the other raised a concrete inch or two,
like neighbors keeping up, as neighbors do.
My poet's thought—intrusive, I suspect—
would like imagination to erect
a library between them, shelves and shelves
of lives in place, communing with themselves.
But no, just once let's go with what we've got:
this cemetery and this parking lot.

CHECKING IT TWICE

"I have more kinfolks on the other side
than this, by now," my mother used to say.
And so it is, and who can turn away
from them because they've died,

though every last departure feels like theft,
each silence like assault? Of course we know
it's no more their own wish to turn and go
than ours to be left,

and every charge is dropped beside the grave
indictment of defection from our love,
but in the living heart they're guilty of
this wound their leaving gave.

What leaves is all we know. Faith swears it wakes
elsewhere, transformed by light not for these eyes;
but we who see by this light say faith lies
with every vow it makes.

Still, kin is kin for good: awake, asleep,
imminent, still far off, all weigh the same
on this long growing roster where we name
the company we keep.

Song

From hair to horse to house to rose,
her tongue unfastened like her gait,
her gaze, her guise, her ghost, she goes.

She cannot name the thing she knows,
word and its image will not mate.
From hair to horse to house to rose

there is a circle will not close.
She babbles to her dinner plate.
All gaze and gaunt as ghost she goes—

smiling at these, frowning at those,
smoothing the air to make it straight—
from hair to horse to house to rose.

She settles in a thoughtful pose
as if she understood her fate,
her face, her gaze, her ghost. She goes

downstream relentlessly, she flows
where dark forgiving waters wait.
From hair to horse to house to rose,
her gaze, her guise, her ghost, she goes.

AGUA

Mother, the trees you loved are dense with water,
alive with wings darting through stippled blue
of recent and imminent rain. And that old street
you mistook for water—remember?—is flowing still,
as when we walked between its banks of pickets
down to the river, which you knew was water
and spoke to, leaning over it last summer.

Mother, those cracks in pavement you stepped over,
avoiding water you imagined, are cradling
eddies of clover, tufted islands of moss;
and look how the roots of that locust are pouring into
every crevice, joining water to water,
look how its trunk is a fountain, a tower of water
out to the tips of its fussy, feathery branches.

Mother, balmy old Thales, how true your sight was
that pierced every disguise, uncovered the water
that links us, the current that bears us
from season to season, whose tide you greeted
in the mindless music you spoke, ocean departing,
returning, into whose keeping, Mother,
you slipped from your body's mooring and out before me.

BY MORNING

The bus taking me god knows where last night
rumbled through rain tracing its cryptic dark
message down dusty windows. At a light
beside the gate to some deserted park,
we stopped; you boarded, with your little boy
giddy and squirming on your breast, sat down
two rows before me. Lit by sudden joy
we moved together now through that wet town,
speaking of nothing much, the tired child
struggling to stay awake, until you left,
turning to wave once, vanished in the wild
beyond our glow as into some black cleft.
You died childless last year at sixty-four.
Useless to wish one could remember more.

For Evan, Who Says I Am Too Tidy

On grandson's lips, "tidy" is pretty dire:
it smacks of age and tameness, of desire
banked by gray prudence, waiting for commands,
forced to endure the scrubbing of both hands.

But tidy sets the table, mends the toys,
lays out clean bedding and such minor joys
as underpin contentment and at least
nourish with daily bread, if not with feast.

Tidy's been blamed for everything we suffer
from guilt to prisons. But free-wheeling's rougher,
less wary not to fracture laws and bones,
much less adept with statutes than with stones.

True, tidy seldom goes where genius goes,
but then how many do? And heaven knows
there's work for us who watch the time, the purse,
the washing of small hands. I've been called worse.

PARA MI TATARANIETO EL ASTROPIONERO

Tú, Fulanito, que por los caminos de mi sangre
te lanzas al futuro, dime si te llevas
los mil sabores del viento, la voz del río,
las lenguas de musgo y helecho que cantan la tierra.

¿Y dónde dejaste la lluvia? Que no se te pierda,
ni el gemir de la gaviota en su desierto azul,
ni esas estrellas tibias como caricias
que no encontrarás en tus noches de acero.

Fíjate que no te falten mariposas;
apréndete el color de las horas;
y toma, que en esta cajita de huesos
te dejo el perfume de los mares.

FOR MY GREAT-GREAT GRANDSON THE SPACE PIONEER

You, What's-your-name, who down the byways of my blood
are hurtling toward the future, tell me if you've packed
the thousand flavors of the wind, the river's voice,
the tongues of moss and fern singing the earth.

And where have you left the rain? Careful: don't lose it,
nor the moan of the seagull in her blue desert,
nor those stars warm as caresses
you will not find again in your nights of steel.

Watch that you don't run short of butterflies;
learn the colors of the hours;
and here, in this little case of bones
I've left you the perfume of the seas.

REVIEW

SESTINA

Wait long enough, and what you need will come:
the rent, acceptance, and now here's *How We Die,*
reviewed, with liberal quotes, in this week's *Times.*
"Heart failure, lung collapse," more, in clear prose,
with nothing softened and no truth left out.
Maybe there's some advice on what to do—

assuming there is something one can do—
not to avoid or hasten what must come
but to uncomplicate the route, get out
with the least fuss. Good title, *How We Die:*
stress on the process, necessary prose,
the work of bodies not our own, but time's.

Scripture, it seems, is right: there are set times,
"inherent limits," within which we do
whatever living means. If zealous pros
armed with contraptions work to overcome
disease, after some brief reprieve we die
because "the taper…simply sputters out."

That's the good news, I guess, if it rules out
the willful tampering, the myth that time's
what we crave, that we fear most to die.
The bad news is that death is hard to do.
Those final moments that we dreamed would come
smooth as remembered poems…are rough prose.

Or so this author says, in doctor-prose
clean as good sutures: "dignity" is out.
But facts (says Proust) never obey us, come
as we least looked for: people, places, times

defeat prediction. Is the thing to do,
then, to forecast the scene in which we die

so luridly that when we come to die
it cannot be just so? Ah, if great prose
were more than words and could both mean and do!
Maybe I'll buy this book, then throw it out
unread; or send this poem to the *Times;*
or ignore death till it decides to come;

or read the damn book; dye my hair; work out;
consult the pros, the tarot; pretend time's
not after me; just do, till Kingdom Come.

BREAD

My daughter-in-law is baking bread for dinner.
The smell of it arabesques through the house like music
and out to the spring-damp lawn where crocuses rear
their helmets of mauve steel from underground.

STEAL?

She wipes the dusting of flour from round arms speckled
with a faint mottling of freckles, peach-colored, rose,
smooths the silk of her auburn hair. We set the table:
her grandmother's blueberry bowl, my mother's crystal.

I picture, as in cartoons, our forbears, tense
on opposite sides of the Channel, fifteen eighty-eight,
Renaissance script in bubbles above their heads:
Spanish war-cries, English curses, the Great Armada.

Remote in their rusty passions now as in armor,
perhaps they dreamed us, but they were like us, living,
afraid of the cannon, afraid the enemy's eyes
would follow them into death as deep as forever.

Blessed be time that closes all eyes, that rouses flowers;
blessed be law that moulds the dust of soldiers
into the bones of daughters, that kneads old strangers
into the flesh of children like braided challah.

DONE WITH MIRRORS

This mirror, and that other, front and side,
conspire to entertain me with a show:
my mother's face in profile, single wide
cheek, broad back, shoulder and breast. But no,
this is myself, preparing for the night,
hairbrush and cloth in hand, and pumice stone;
still, for one instant, clear in borrowed light
my mother's flesh resolves into my own.

Is this a trick of wishing, love or glass
leading the eye to find itself again,
the lip to kiss, to bless, the hand to pass
over lost faces? Or do women, men
crowd all our mirrors, as someday we, too,
may rise into your light, your mirror, you?

VOYEUR

A man is at the window in a room
you have no need to visit. Shoulder, face,
black undershirt; beside him, in the gloom,
a tiny leaping light you barely trace
back to a screen, unwatched. He watches you
instead. And you stare back, brazen behind
your flimsy namelessness. What would you do,
you think, if he stepped through this parted blind,
yanked you out of the safety of your skin
into his cage of hours, his alien wild
memory like tattoos? Or what if, in
some flowering complicity, you smiled
across the falling night? He looks about;
you shut the blinds to keep the darkness out.

RAINY SUNDAY

"What are you thinking?" he asked. We had not spoken.
"Nothing," I said, and it was partly true,
For thought was not the silence he had broken,
But slow rains drifting earthward. Cold and blue,
A dog was barking in my memory...
Another...and another. My sad town
Filtered its tattered twilight over me;
Regrets, like odors, sifted softly down
And blew the world away. He could not know
That in a web of lamplight, as in bars
I was a child caught in the long ago
And pinioned to the wake of alien stars.
The dead were with me, chanting their old wrongs,
Scratchy with use, trapped in a dusty groove.
Far off I heard the present sing its songs
And watched the world retreat, and could not move.
Fearful at last, and hungry for my kind,
I thrust the dead away by force of will
And sighed, how blessed it is to leave behind
All but this living world that knows me still!
And then I saw his eyes, opaque with thought
And dark with silences where I was not.

ROACH

A leggy speck, a fleck of brown
caught flicking on the rim of sight:
when he saw me, it must have been
apocalypse by reading light.

A jolt of current triggered by
nothing so convolute as grief—
and yet so like despair I winced—
flattened his body like a leaf,

snapped back his pinhead face to stare
at landscape hugely gone awry,
electrified him out of choice
and gave him barely time to die.

I clubbed him with the nearest book.
I've heard the cells that help them tense
are so like ours that microscopes
can barely tell the difference.

RESERVATION

As if he has decided on a nap
but feels too pressed for time to find his bed
or even shift the napkin from his lap,
the man across the table drops his head
mid-anecdote, just managing to clear
a basket of warm rolls and butter stacked
like little golden dice beside his ear.
The lady seems embarrassed to attract
such swift attention from the formal stranger
who leaves his dinner, bends as if to wake
the sleeper, seeks a pulse. Others arrange her
coat about her, gather round to take
the plates, the quiet form, her name, her hand.
Now slowly she begins to understand.

THE PRODIGAL SON GOES OVER NOTES FOR HIS MEMOIRS

Dredging up this and that forgotten bit
of vanished finery and rare old wine,
those nights that drained my wallet and my wit,
those foreign tarts for whom I cannot pine
(but should, in this church-picnic neighborhood!)
I mull over that harvest of wild oats
gathered while my brother, silent, good,
wept by the old man's bed and fed the goats.
But how confess the worst for him to read?
His bitterness, his envy, his despair,
are all he has, all of me he may need,
to justify the ashes in his hair.
Why scourge him with a truth less truth than taunt,
how little in the world there is to want?

Swinging an Arc Before Him As He Goes

Swinging an arc before him as he goes,
the blind man claims his slice of pie, his cane
tapping the crust. In there, the world is sane;
outside—not his affair—he must suppose
anything possible. As the pie grows,
all streets, with what they promise and contain,
become just barely his. He must not feign
wider acquaintance than the slice he knows.

The blind man lives by four, and we by five,
but senses are just senses, and perhaps
less to be trusted than the hungry drive
compelling him along the route he takes.
And luck, which is the same, whether one makes
a stab at seeing, or one swings and taps.

GRAVIDA

Look how she tilts, self-loving and sedate
as a small ship riding a painted storm:
forward and back at once she bears her freight,
tentative in big boots. I picture, warm
in her young body, how the child is curled,
oblivious of December, traffic, sleet,
the blown useless umbrella, night, the world,
as she maneuvers both across the street.
I make an effort—less of memory
than of old muscles—to remember how
the same blood-heavy wisdom once taught me
to love my body more than I do now,
to move for what I carried day by day,
to tilt into the storm a while, her way.

WEIGHING IN

What the scale tells you is how much the earth
has missed you, body, how it wants you back
again after you leave it to go forth

into the light. Do you remember how
earth hardly noticed you then? Others would rock
you in their arms, warm in the flow

that fed you, coaxed you upright. Then earth began
to claim you with spots and fevers, began to lick
at you with a bruised knee, a bloody shin,

and finally to stroke you, body, drumming
intimate coded messages through music
you danced to unawares, there in your dreaming

and your poems and your obedient blood.
Body, how useful you became, how lucky,
heavy with news and breakage, rich, and sad,

sometimes, imagining that greedy zero
you must have been, that promising empty sack
of possibilities, never-to-come tomorrow.

But look at you now, body, soft old shoe
that love wears when it's stirring, look down, look
how earth wants what you weigh, needs what you know.

INTERLUDE

Say that a happy woman at that stage
given to counted blessings counts them now
not to be comforted, not to assuage
vague disappointment, but to watch them bow
before memory's curtains as they close
on this good Second Act. There's more ahead,
but what—and how it ends—nobody knows.
Say she recites what those old players said
who made her laugh and vanished with Act One;
Listens for exit lines as yet unheard
although foreshadowed, as the deed undone
cries out in retrospect; mouths every word,
long-wished-for or long-feared or still to say,
before the last applause has died away.

How It Begins

Somebody's blade fingers your chest,
out for the bird in its warm nest
rocked in those tides that come and go.
Somebody's thumb is on the flow
memory rides through secret places
to find the doors, to name the faces.
Somebody's picking body's lock,
tapping the glass, hefting a rock,
leaping the gate, cutting the wire
that fuses motion to desire.
What if this once nobody's there?
Somebody's step is on the stair.

RACHMANINOFF ON THE MASS PIKE

It calls the heart, this music, to a place
more intimate than home, than self, that face
aging in the hall mirror. This is not
music to age by—no sprightly gavotte
or orderly pavane, counting each beat,
confining motion to the pointed feet
and sagely nodding head; not Chopin, wise
enough to keep some distance in his eyes
between perceiver and the thing perceived.
No, this is song that means to be believed,
that quite believes itself, each rising wave
of passionate crescendo wild and brave.
The silly girl who lived inside my skin
once loved this music; its melodic din
was like the voice she dreamed in, sad, intense.
She didn't know a thing, she had no sense;
she scorned—and needed—calendar and clock,
the rules, the steps, the lines, Sebastian Bach;
she wanted life to break her like a tide—
but not too painfully. On either side
the turnpike trundles by, nurseries, farms,
small towns with schools and markets in their arms,
small industry, green spaces now and then.
All the heart wants is to be called again.

SUBSISTENCE

How like a child balking at some new dish
you turn, heart, from your plate and will not taste!
Useless to tempt you—spoon now bird, now fish,
now sailboat in mid-air, its cargo laced
with sugared patience—coaxing yes and yes
for this or that inexorable loss,
smiling, crooning in praise of less and less.
You scowl for what there was, arrogant, cross,
as if you had been rich once. Look how mind
scurries to bargain for what's left, makes do
with what there is, knows how to scrape the rind
and sweeten it with hunger, working to
educate the palate to relent
so as to feed on stones and be content.

Sixty-Five

You want the truth? Disaster. How they flew,
those early decades! What I would, I might,
or so I thought, sure of just who was who
and what was what. But age has dimmed the light.
Picture my neurons: what a tangled fright,
all fitful sparks in memory's trackless fen,
half way to tabula rasa, blank and white!
It's not a year I'd care to do again.

My body hates me. And it's mutual, too.
We never speak these days except to fight.
There's less and less I like it still can do.
My bladder yells at me; my clothes are tight.
I loathe these dewlaps and these jowls that blight
the profile boys would notice, way back when.
I'm sagging gentle into that good night.
It's not a year I'd care to do again.

Those supermarket Romeos make me blue,
dim widowers who ask me to recite
my recipes from memory. It's true
I'm touched by their wan smiles, and they don't bite,
with or without their dentures. Ah, the flight
of hours I danced away! But that was then.
Look what's become of that young, rosy sprite.
It's not a year I'd care to do again.

Poet, you praised the ageless, hard and bright;
you said this is no country for old men—
or women either—and you got that right.
It's not a year I'd care to do again.

Brown

Brown of the sparrow hopping where seeds lie,
of the fat woodchuck foraging, and brown
of marsh in April mirroring the sky.
Brown of my mother's eyes, of my still town
in heavy rains; of rust; of nested down
long after flight; of chocolate on chill nights
when I was young; of oak; of pews; of crown
around God's wounded brow by altar lights;
of log in the cold hearth the match ignites
like memory; of dried blood on a sheet;
of names on a long list the stone recites;
brown of the earth that waits, stroking the feet;
brown of late shadows gathering, of loam,
of that first sleep, of rest, of going home.

SEQUEL

"Hope is the thing with feathers
That perches in the soul..."

—Emily Dickinson

What bird it was that sang me through the cold
I know, Emily, and just how bleak the night
its feathered willfulness contrived to hold
at bay with nothing. Then, in failing light,
it sang out of my need, and never grieved
at all, driven to daring, unresigned;
it sang me promises, and I believed,
though evidence was slight and hard to find.
Emily, tell the sequel: find me, please,
that bird in hiding now that summer's come
to ripen fruit, to slow the pulse with ease,
to bring the banners down and still the drum,
these days when all is well and nothing sings
out of the smooth finality of things.

SACRAMENT

Touch any stranger, and the face turned smiling
toward you will be familiar, will be your father
miraculously clear of the dust he sleeps in,
your mother, stylish again; spot any driver
tapping the wheel at a light, and it will be
your son's quick profile flicking into traffic.

But no, not really: behind those mock encounters
lie real departures, past or to come. Some
gesture invites you, but then the eyes are wrong,
off-colored, angled oddly, so memory stumbles,
as you may stumble at dawn down a hallway,
fumble at a knob, wonder what place this is,

What became of the stairway that used to rise here.
And then a face floats toward you over a trickle
of water, where you wash, as if you were meeting
at a shallow river, as if you had come to be given
the name you will need by morning, as if
you were summoned home every day to this touch.

OCCUPATIONAL HAZARD

You may hide out in prose, as others do,
when circumstances say it's time to lie,
but what you sing is certain to be true.

I've known that all my life; it's nothing new.
A poem tells it straight—I don't know why.
It will not watch your back, as prose can do,

or be a mask to speak around or through,
or script an alibi; don't even try,
since what it sings is never less than true.

Prose thinks before it speaks, plans how to sue,
dazzle, amaze, amuse, evade, deny;
unlike this song, it knows just what to do.

These very lines won't lift a finger to
dress themselves with more than truth can buy.
Sing, and against your will you sing it true.

I sing you this because it's meant for you
and I would have your trust until I die.
Yes, I can trim my prose—it's what we do.
But what I sing, believe. You know that's true.

INVOCATION

Goddess, mother, mentor of those who live to
scribble verses, now in my seventh decade
reaping scanty laurels for minor triumphs,
Muse, I entreat you:

Do not slight me, lady who never failed me
then, in youth, when, stolen from mop and bucket,
merest seconds spent in your rites once brought me
sound of your timbrels.

Image, music, memory, mind's reflection:
let these now, as then, in the freight of each day
seem enough to treasure without betraying
moment to meaning.

Keep me truthful, grant that I never sing it
trendy, bending messages to their hearers,
louder, higher, stranger than speech would have it,
pitching for pennies.

Slap my hand hard, goddess, if once you catch me
reaching out for glory and those Big Prizes;
spare me, after reading the lists of Winners,
poisonous envy,

rage, excuses, rancorous grief and sniping.
Teach me you are singing in all those voices,
not in this or that one more than another's.
Teach me my one voice;

Teach me to work keeping it just my measure,
narrow, rooted, bound to the gift you lent me,
simple as dirt, useful as broom and ladle,
needle and trowel.

INTERVIEW WITH A POLTERGEIST

No, nothing left behind, no debt, no kiss
denied and hankered for. It's what I do,
that's all. Why do I do it? Let's just say
one's work, like love, defies analysis.
Hunters after the beautiful and true,
for instance, may deny their work is play
but play it is. I work—for meager pay,
by living standards that apply to you—
but I am both above those, and below.
How do I choose a home? Easy: where too
much light almost obscures the fact that this
contradicts that, belief whispers "Not so"
behind the flowered wallpaper, I go
to fling the books. And where do you live, Miss?

READING VERMEER

"The poet," says the poet, "strives to ask
not more, but other. He works alone, outside.
Risk is the fuel he runs on, and his pride
is harnessed to his task."

But I must beg (outsiders do, and thrive!)
to differ. For example, read Vermeer,
whose people, drenched in light, like honey, wear
the blessing of the hive.

No sullen, driving, arbitrary hill
grudges his flat world its serenity
or mocks the decent soul to wrench it free
of maps that hold it still.

Framed by her room, pleased for acquaintance's sake,
this woman reads a letter: nothing new.
The other pours, glad of what's left to do,
glad of her bread to bake.

Of course, I could be wrong:
both may be adding up their model's wages,
and mine the only poem on these pages
to celebrate a life that slows to song.

PARALLAX

I never write the words I meant to write.
Those come from where I've been, looking for me;
they are a door ajar, as if they might
almost be true, and almost make me free.
But then the words that they set out to be
become those others that perhaps I meant
for naming what I wanted not to see,
as if some truth half giving its consent
turned, and the turning made it different
and led it elsewhere, somehow, by a hand
not the same hand that guided my intent.
I mean to write those words I understand
before they speak themselves, but then they close.
And what they would have said, god only knows.

CLASS NOTES

I had a student once who couldn't write.
Well, one of many. But this boy was bright,
fizzing with thoughts he felt he had to clothe
in verses, if you please! And I was loath
to stem a tide so eager in its flow.
We bent over his work together: "No,"
I'd say, "a little tighter here, a little less
would make it stronger." I did not say "mess"
or crumple anything; I never laughed.
He followed me for days, draft after draft
waved in my face, hopeful and typed and clean,
for proud use in our student magazine.
"Yes, fine," I sighed at last, "this we can use,
not bad." Which wasn't true. That night the Muse
turned up beside my desk, leafed through our journal
with scathing looks. The Muse is not maternal,
not given to be flexible or gentle
with man or boy. She calls that sentimental.
Once language is debased and craft forgotten,
she hissed, the fabric of all speech goes rotten.
How dare I, she went on, who swore to live
under her strictures, fracture them to give
praise in her name to work so undeserving?
By morning I had vowed to be unswerving
in my devotion henceforth. And the test
came soon: shy, slight, neither the worst nor best
in a slow class, colorless, not a child
to be remembered long, she had a mild
aptitude for a flabby line or two.
But I was chastened now: "These will not do
for print just yet," I wrote her in red pen.
"Work on them; in September, try again."

58

By summer she was gone to foster care.
She'd wept behind her hand. I had been fair,
the Muse was pleased with me; the saints were not.
Saints, largely an unliterary lot,
apply the hair shirt skillfully, and boast
more tongues of flame than any Holy Ghost.
I've heard them all by now, and come no nearer
to answers either just or kind or clearer
than I had then, still fail to make an end
of war between firm teacher and soft friend,
hard fact, well-meaning lie, injury, touch,
what truth is worth and why it costs so much.

BILINGUAL/BILINGÜE

My father liked them separate, one there,
one here (allá y aquí), as if aware

that words might cut in two his daughter's heart
(el corazón) and lock the alien part

to what he was—his memory, his name
(su nombre)—with a key he could not claim.

"English outside this door, Spanish inside,"
he said, "y basta." But who can divide

the world, the word (mundo y palabra) from
any child? I knew how to be dumb

and stubborn (testaruda); late, in bed,
I hoarded secret syllables I read

until my tongue (mi lengua) learned to run
where his stumbled. And still the heart was one.

I like to think he knew that, even when,
proud (orgulloso) of his daughter's pen,

he stood outside mis versos, half in fear
of words he loved but wanted not to hear.

POETRY READING

Admit it: you're here against your will.
Somebody made you come; somebody said
you need a break from watching people kill
people on TV, or count the dead
in Bosnia. Or you came to hear us tease
meaning from accident; I wish you luck.
I saw a man stalk out of one of these
recently, all incensed: he had been struck
by human conversation, by the sound
of strangers speaking, not to history,
but to each other. And he had not found
"the world," he said—whatever that may be—
in poems read that evening. And he missed it.
Well, you've been warned: whatever world you came
to find or curse or grieve may not be listed
in our small menu, whose dishes wear the name
of local spots. Here is a wedding ring,
for instance, and a son, a death or two,
crows on a fence, the sea, some secret thing
whose skin I found, the Virgin Mary—who
knows what else. It's random, home-made fare.
Stay; you may like it. Find yourself a chair.

FOR THE FRIEND WHO GUIDED ME HOME FROM A POETRY READING, THROUGH TRAFFIC, ON UNFAMILIAR ROADS

No, it's no use: the map is in my hand,
but nothing in it matches what the land
invents at every turn. I stop the car,
abashed, to say I don't know where we are.
But you reword the landscape, resolute,
with one audacious finger trace a route
as you might trim a phrase or shift a tense
to smooth the beat or clarify the sense;
you signal me to follow. I think Troy
burning, and Aeneas, that brave boy,
bowed with his father's weight on his young back,
headed for Rome; I think the railroad track,
some hapless maiden chained to it, unbound
one breath before the engine's horrid sound.
Allusion to allusion leads, and now—
throat dry, white-knuckled, sweat on my cold brow—
I see you turning sharply, blinking right,
like Virgil shining through the Stygian night,
and think Inferno and the coils of Hell.
But no, it's Route 110, and all is well:
your rear-view mirror wears your smiling face,
and one hand waving puts the world in place.
One bridge to cross, and soon—it seems a minute—
my own front door, with my own husband in it!
Now, bliss—well, coffee, anyway—chitchat
about some prize, this editor and that;
lines to be scanned in novel ways that change
familiar meanings into something strange
but maybe truer than what custom saw;
the pull between mute nature and the law

we burden and enrich her with, through speech;
those timeless mermaids singing each to each;
and—change of weather now—a touch of Frost.
Who would not risk being a little lost
to be at last so well and wisely found?
But now the sun, that brings the planet round
to order in twelve stanzas, morn to eve,
begins its dying fall, and you must leave.
Regretful at the door I wave you on;
your taillights flicker left, and soon you're gone.
Cartographer whose lines sing to the mind
so clear, so sure that they could guide the blind
through wilderness, may all your journeys end,
like mine today, home safe with a good friend.

"Why Publish?"

Dusty and brown on some forgotten shelf
a century hence—or two, let dreams be grand!—
this wry and slanted gloss upon myself
has slipped into some stranger's browsing hand.
A woman, maybe, growing old like me,
or a young man ambitious for his name,
curious about my antique prosody
but pleased to find our motives much the same.
He cannot know—nor she—what this one life
from the late twentieth craved, or cost, or found;
he will forget my name; but mother, wife,
daughter, has struck a chord, sings from the ground
a moment to his ear, as now to yours,
for what is ours in common and endures.

AFTERWORD

Bilingual/Bilingüe

RECENT INTEREST in the phenomenon known as "Spanglish" has led me to reexamine my own experience as a writer who works chiefly in her second language, and especially to recall my father's inflexible rule against the mixing of languages. In fact, no English was allowed in that midtown Manhattan apartment that became home after my arrival in New York in 1939. My father read the daily paper in English, taught himself to follow disturbing events in Europe through the medium of English-language radio, and even taught me to read the daily comic strips, in an effort to speed my learning of the language he knew I would need. But that necessary language was banished from family conversation: it was the medium of the outer world, beyond the door; inside, among ourselves, only Spanish was permitted, and it had to be pure, grammatical, unadulterated Spanish.

At the age of seven, however, nothing seems more important than communicating with classmates and neighborhood children. For my mother, too, the new language was a way out of isolation, a means to deal with the larger world and with those American women for whom she sewed. But my father, a political exile waiting for changes in our native country, had different priorities: he lived in the hope of return, and believed that the new home, the new speech, were temporary. His theory was simple: if it could be said at all, it could be said best in the language of those authors whose words were the core of his education. But his insistence on pure Spanish made it difficult, sometimes impossible, to bring home and share the jokes of friends, puns, pop lyrics, and other staples of seven-year-old conversation. Table talk sometimes ended with tears or sullen silence.

And yet, despite the friction it caused from time to time, my native language was also a source of comfort—the reading that I loved, intimacy within the family, and a peculiar auditory delight best described as echoes in the mind. I learned early to relish words

67

as counters in a game that could turn suddenly serious without losing the quality of play, and to value their sound as a meaning behind their meaning.

Nostalgia, a confusion of identity, the fear that if the native language is lost the self will somehow be altered forever: all are part of the subtle flavor of immigrant life, as well as the awareness that one owes gratitude to strangers for acts of communication that used to be simple and once imposed no such debt.

Memory, folklore, and food all become part of the receding landscape that language sets out to preserve. Guilt, too, adds to the mix, the suspicion that to love the second language too much is to betray those ancestors who spoke the first and could not communicate with us in the vocabulary of our education, our new thoughts. And finally, a sense of grievance and loss may spur hostility toward the new language and those who speak it, as if the common speech of the perceived majority could weld together a disparate population into a huge, monolithic, and threatening Other. That Other is then assigned traits and habits that preclude sympathy and mold "Us" into a unity whose cohesiveness gives comfort.

Luckily, there is another side to bilingualism: curiosity about the Other may be as natural and pervasive as group loyalty. If it weren't, travel, foreign residence, and intermarriage would be less common than they are. For some bilingual writers, the Other—and the language he speaks—are appealing. Some acknowledge and celebrate the tendency of languages to borrow from each other and produce something different in the process. That is, in part, the tendency that has given rise to "Spanglish."

It's dangerous, however, to accept the inevitable melding of languages over time as a justification for speaking, in the short run, a mix that impoverishes both languages by allowing words in one to drive out perfectly good equivalent words in the other. The habitual speaker of such a mix ends by speaking not two, or even one complete language, but fragments of two that are no longer capable of standing alone or serving the speaker well with any larger audience. As a literary device with limited appeal and durability, "Spanglish," like other such blends, is expressive and fresh. But as a substitute for genuine bilinguality—the cultivation and preservation of two languages—I suspect it represents a danger to the advancement of foreign speakers, and a loss to both cultures. My father sensed as much in 1939, and stubbornly preserved my native language for me, through his insistence that I be truly bilingual rather than a traveler across boundaries that "Spanglish" has made all too permeable.

My father, who never learned to think in English, was persuaded that the words of his own language were the "true" names for things in the world. But for me that link between fact and word was broken, as it is for many who grow up bilingual. Having been taught to love words and take them seriously as reflections of reality, I felt it a loss to learn that, in fact, words are arbitrary, man-made, no more permanent than clothing: somewhere under all of them reality is naked.

Disconcerting as it is, however, to lose the security of words that are perceived as single keys to what they unlock, it is also exhilarating to see oneself as the maker of those words, even if they are now impermanent, provisional artifacts that have value for us only because they're ours. Anybody who has ever gone hunting for that one right and elusive word knows what bilingualism feels like, even if he's never left his native country or learned a word in any language but his own. There is a sense in which every poet is bilingual, and those of us who are more overtly so are only living metaphors for the condition that applies to us all. We use a language that seems deceptively like the language of the people around us, but isn't quite. The words are the same, but the weight we give them, the connections we find among them, the criteria we use to choose this one rather than that one, are our own.

At a recent poetry reading I closed with a poem in Spanish, and a member of the English-speaking audience approached me afterward to remark how moved she had been by that poem, and how she wished I had read others.

"Where did you learn Spanish?" I asked.

"I don't speak any Spanish," she replied. "What I understood was the music of what you read."

It occurred to me, during our subsequent conversation, that poetry may be precisely what is almost lost, not in translation, but in the wording, the transit from experience to paper. If we succeed in salvaging anything, maybe it is most often in the music, the formal elements of poetry that do travel from language to language, as the formal music of classic Spanish poetry my father loved followed me into English and draws me, to this day, to poems that are patterned and rich and playful.

It's occurred to me since that conversation that a poem in Spanish may have more in common with a poem in English—or any other language—than with a grocery list, say, or a piece of technical writing that happens to use Spanish words. There is something in poetry that transcends specific language, that makes it possible for transplanted people like me to recognize the songs of the Other as his own even before he understands them fully. Poetry may be used to draw very small circles around itself, identifying its speaker as a member of a narrowly delineated group and looking at "outsiders" with eyes that discern less and less detail as distance increases. But it may also be used to draw very large circles, circles that will draw in rather than exclude, as in Edwin Markham's apt four-line metaphor titled "Outwitted":

> He drew a circle that shut me out—
> Heretic, rebel, a thing to flout.
> But Love and I had the wit to win:
> We drew a circle that shut him in.

About the Author

Born in the Dominican Republic in 1932, Rhina P. Espaillat has lived in the U.S. since 1939 and writes chiefly in English, but occasionally also in her native Spanish. Her work appears frequently in anthologies and magazines; she has won numerous awards, most recently from *Sparrow, Blue Unicorn* and *Medicinal Purposes,* as well as several from *Orbis,* The World Order of Narrative and Formalist Poets, and The Poetry Society of America.

Design and typography by Timothy Rolands
Cover design by Timothy Rolands and Teresa Wheeler

The poems and text are set in ITC Legacy Serif,
a revival of Nicolas Jenson's excellent roman,
designed by Ronald Arnholm.
Some display text is set in Mantinia,
designed by Matthew Carter.

This book was printed and bound
by Thomson-Shore, Dexter, Michigan.